We the People

THE ALABAMA DUI HANDBOOK FOR JUSTICE

◆

Roderick Van Daniel, Ph. D. & J.D.

Van Daniel Marketing, LLC
Aberdeen Birmingham Memphis Atlanta

THE ALABAMA DUI HANDBOOK FOR JUSTICE

Van Daniel Marketing, LLC

For information address:
Van Daniel Marketing, LLC
vandanielmarketing@hotmail.com
www.vandanielmarketing.webs.com

Printed in the United States of America

"I will continue my journey of going to court to speak for those who cannot speak for themselves, knowing that in some venues the blindfold of Lady Justice drops below one eye so that she (Justice) sees the badge and gun on one side and sees the accused citizen on the other. Justice not 'blinded' is not just. Therefore, I press on representing citizens accused of driving under the influence (DUI). This is my privilege."

   - *Phillip B. Price, Sr.,* Attorney at Law

"Truth is always strong, no matter how weak it looks, and falsehood is always weak no matter how strong it looks."

   - *Marcus Antonius*

"One can stand as the greatest orator the world has known, possess the quickest mind, employ the cleverest psychology, and have mastered all the technical devices of argument, but if one is not credible one might just as well preach to the pelicans."

   - *Gerry Spence,* Attorney at Law

Contents

◆

For my mother,
Yvonne Daniel

Acknowledgement
◆

This handbook is dedicated to the citizens of Alabama that need help to fight against their injustices. A number of citizens need assistance with fighting and learning about driving under the influence (DUI). This information is here to serve you and thank you for reading the Alabama DUI Handbook for Justice. This handbook will be an ongoing process.

The Law of DUI

The Law of DUI

Living through another bad situation......

    You just received your first DUI and you are afraid. You never have been in a situation like this before. You have a family, career, respectable citizen in the community, and tonight you just had too many drinks. You are extremely lost and do not know what to do.

    Well, the purpose of this handbook is to help relieve some of your worries and to provide the citizens of Alabama who are seeking justice with information relating to the laws, statutes, rules, and regulations regarding the subject of driving under the influence (DUI). Specifically, the handbook will address the field sobriety tests, sentences range based on prior convictions, the 10 Day Limit, and ways to get out of a DUI. So, what is a DUI?

Generally, driving under the influence (DUI) is the offense of operating a motor vehicle in a physically or mentally impaired condition after consuming alcohol or drugs. In Alabama, the DUI statute prohibited not just driving, but being in actual physical control of any vehicle while under the influence. A person in actual physical control of a vehicle has a present ability to drive, move, or steer the vehicle in some manner, such that a serious potential risk of physical injury to another exists. U.S. v. McGill, 347 F.Supp. 2d 1210 (M.D. Ala. 2004). A person maybe convicted of (DUI) who is in actual physical control of his vehicle, but not yet driving; even when he is asleep in his parked vehicle. Raley v. State, 586 So. 2d 285 (Ala. Crim. App. 1991). In other words, it is not required that one be actually driving a vehicle in order to be found guilty of violating the (DUI) statute. Adams v. State. 585 So. 2d 156 (Ala. Crim. App. 1991).

The vast majority of DUI cases usually involve trucks, automobiles, SUVs, and motorcycles. However, in Alabama according to the Alabama Code provides that bicycles, horses, riding lawn movers, animal driven wagons, mules, and tractors driven by a person can commit DUI. Ala. Code § 32-1-1.1(81). So, what is the DUI statute that changes the lives of the citizens of Alabama and everywhere in our country?

In Alabama, the law for **DUI** is found in the Alabama Code 1975 § 32-5A-191. Driving while under influence of alcohol, controlled substances, etc.:

a. A person **shall not** drive or be in actual physical control of any vehicle while:

1. There is 0.08 % or more by weight of alcohol in his or her blood:

2. Under the influence of alcohol;

3. Under the influence of controlled substance to a degree which renders him or her incapable of safely driving;

4. Under the combined influence of alcohol and a controlled substance to a degree which renders him or her incapable of safely driving; or

5. Under the influence of any substance which impairs the mental or physical faculties of such person to a degree which renders him or her incapable of safely driving.

b. A person who is under the age of 21 years **shall not** drive or be in actual control of any vehicle if there is 0.02 percent or more by weight of alcohol in his or her blood. The Department of Public Safety shall suspend or revoke the driver's license of any person, including, but not limited to, a juvenile, child, or youthful offender, convicted or adjudicated of, or subjected to a finding of, delinquency based on this subsection. Notwithstanding the foregoing, upon the first violation of this subsection by <u>a person whose blood alcohol level is between 0.02 and 0.08, the person's driver's license or driving privilege shall be suspended for a period of 30 days</u> in lieu of any penalties provided in subsection (e) of this section, and there shall be no disclosure, other than to courts, law enforcement agencies, and the person's employer, by any entity or person of any information, documents, or records relating to the person's arrest, conviction, adjudication of or finding of delinquency based on this subsection. <u>All persons</u>, except as otherwise provided in this subsection for a first offense, including, but not limited to, a juvenile, child, or youthful offender, convicted or adjudicated of or subjected to a finding of delinquency based on this subsection shall be fined pursuant to this section, notwithstanding any other to the contrary, and the person shall also be required to attend and complete a DUI or substance abuse court referral program in accordance with subsection (k).

c.　(1) A <u>school bus or day care driver</u> **shall not** drive or be in actual physical control of any vehicle while in performance of his or her duties if there <u>is greater than</u>

0.02 percent by weight of alcohol in his or her blood. A person convicted pursuant to this subsection shall be subject to the penalties provided by this section, except that on the first conviction the Director of Public Safety shall suspend the driving privilege or driver's license for a period of one year.

(2) A person **shall not** drive or be in actual physical control of a commercial motor vehicle, as defined in 49 CFR Part 383.5 of the Federal Motor Carrier Safety Regulations as adopted pursuant to Section 32-9A-2, if there is 0.04 percent or greater by weight of alcohol in his or her blood. Notwithstanding the other provisions of this section, the commercial driver's license or commercial driving privilege of a person convicted of violating this subdivision shall be disqualified for the period provided in accordance with 49 CFR Part 383.51, as applicable, and the person's regular driver's license or privilege to drive a regular motor vehicle shall be governed by the remainder of this section if the person is guilty of a violation of another provision of this section.

d.   The fact that any person charged with violating (DUI) this section is or has been legally entitled to use alcohol or a controlled substance shall not constitute a defense against any charge of violating this section.

DUI Conviction (sentencing ranges) § 32-5A-191

Personally, I know as a citizen receiving a DUI you would to know what will happen to you for your first DUI or even subsequent convictions of DUI. Is it a misdemeanor or felony? This section will cater to your questions about this issue.

First Conviction (Misdemeanor)

A person violating the DUI statute shall be punished by imprisonment in the county or municipal jail for not more than 1 year, or by fine of not less than six hundred dollars ($600) nor more than two thousand one hundred dollars ($2,100), or by both a fine and imprisonment. Also, the DUI defendant will have his driver's license (privileges) suspended for 90 days and will have to attend a court approved substance abuse program.

In Alabama, the "wash out" period for DUI is 5 years. In other words, this means that if a person has only one prior DUI, and the day that he is convicted of his second DUI is more than 5 years after the date of conviction for his first DUI, he will be sentenced within the range of punishment as a first offender. However, if the second DUI conviction is within 5 years of the first conviction he will be punished as a second offense.

Second Conviction (Misdemeanor)

A person convicted within a 5 year period for DUI shall be punished by a fine of not less than ($1,100) nor more than ($5,100) and by imprisonment, which may include hard labor in the county or municipal jail for not more than 1 year. The sentence shall include a mandatory sentence of imprisonment for not less than 5 days or community service for not less than 30 days. The defendant driver's license will be suspended for 1 year, and he will be required to attend a court ordered treatment program.

Third Conviction (Misdemeanor)

A person convicted within a 5 year period for DUI shall be punished by a fine of not less than ($2,100) nor more than ($10,100) and by imprisonment, which may include hard labor, in the county or municipal jail for not less than 60 days nor more than 1 year. The defendant driver's license will be suspended for 3 years and shall be required to complete a court ordered treatment program.

Fourth conviction or more (Class C felony)

A person convicted within a 5 year period of DUI shall be guilty of a Class C felony and punished by a fine of not less than ($4,100) nor more than ($10,100) and by imprisonment of not less than 1 year and 1 day nor more than 10 years. The defendant driver's license will be suspended for 5 years and shall be required to attend a court appointed substance program.

Other penalties of DUI

The other DUI penalties include an ignition interlock device, which is a breath-testing machine attached to the steering wheel of your car, and prevents it from being crank (started) or driven when there is any kind of alcohol in your body.

When a person convicted of DUI is found to have had at least 0.15 percent of more by weight of alcohol in his or her blood while operating or being in actual physical control of a vehicle, he or she shall be sentenced to at least double the minimum punishment that the person would have received if he or she had less than 0.15 percent by weight of alcohol in his or her blood. If the adjudicated offense is a misdemeanor, the minimum punishment shall be imprisonment for 1 year, all of which may be suspended except as otherwise provided by the code of (f) and (g). The defendant driver's license shall be revoke for a period of not less than 1 year.

When a person over the age of 21 years is convicted of DUI and it is found that a child under the age of 14 years was present in the vehicle at the time of the offense, the person shall be sentenced to at least double the minimum punishment that the person would have received if the child had not been present in the motor vehicle.

Also, a person who has been arrested for DUI shall not be released from jail under bond until there is less than the same percent by weight of alcohol in his or her blood.

Furthermore, upon notice that a defendant arrested is currently on probation from another court of this state as a result of a conviction for any criminal offense, the prosecutor shall provide written or oral notification of the defendant's subsequent arrest and pending prosecution to the court in which the prior conviction occurred. Remember after getting a DUI, the **10 Day Limit** will be impose. This is an action that needs to be taken immediately to preserve your privilege to drive. The 10 Day Limit action needs to take place within 10 days from the date of your arrest.

Ways to Avoid A DUI

Ways to Avoid A DUI

I know just you sitting there thinking; how can I avoid even getting a DUI? I do not want to face the penalties of driving drunk according to the laws of Alabama. Here, is a list of suggestions that may help you on your quest to not be a victim of this crime. These are only tips.

1. **SIMPLY DO NOT DRIVE AFTER DRINKING OR USING DRUGS OF ANY KIND.** You can keep it simple for yourself by not driving. Use someone to be your designated driver. Call a friend, cab, family member, or the love of your life to pick you up. Just do not get behind the wheel after consuming alcohol.

2. **KNOW THE LEGAL LIMIT FOR CONSUMPTION OF ALCOHOL.** I know you want to have fun and enjoy life but reality is that driving while intoxicated or even a little tipsy will calculate you over the legal limit. Even though it is not illegal to drink alcohol and drive an automobile; it is illegal to be over the legal limit and drive. Know your limit.

3. **KNOW THE RULES OF THE ROAD.** Remember, the most minor traffic infraction and or equipment violation on your vehicle will give a police officer probable cause to pull you over to check your status. For example, not using a turn signal, having your high beams on, improper lane usage will cause the police officer to pull you over; then next thing you know it leads to a DUI investigation and arrest.

4. **BE POLITE, COURTEOUS, AND RESPECTFUL TO THE POLICE.** It is always good to be a respectable citizen to the police officer but that does not mean tell them everything without asking for an attorney first.

5. **HAVE YOUR DRIVER LICENSE, INSURANCE, AND REGISTRATION AVAILABLE.** This is very important at roadblocks and checkpoints.

6. **UNDERSTAND THAT YOU CAN BE CONVICTED OF DUI IN ALABAMA EVEN IF YOU HAVE NOT CONSUMED ANY ALCOHOL.** Remember, even using a legal prescription applies as a controlled substances and alcohol. Also, other substances like glue, over the counter medications, and including paint can cause you to be charged with a DUI.

7. **DO NOT BE IN ACTUAL PHYSICAL CONTROL OF YOUR VEHICLE.** It would be best for you to fall asleep on passenger side or back seat than under the wheel of the car even if you are parked and asleep.

8. **UNDERSTAND FIELD SOBRIETY TESTS.** No law in Alabama mandates that a person driving a vehicle must submit to the police roadside field sobriety tests. The tests are truly VOLUNTARY. But understanding of why they are given is important.

9. **UNDERSTAND BLOOD ALCOHOL TESTING.** If you are arrested for DUI in Alabama and was driving on a public highway at the time of your arrest, you have consented to submit to a blood alcohol test. Three types in Alabama: a) urine, b) blood, and c) breath.

10. **IF ARRESTED FOR DUI DON NOT PLEAD GUILTY AND HIRE A LAWYER WHO WILL BE DEVOTED TO DEFENDING YOU AGAINST THE DUI CHARGE.**

Tests for DUI

Tests for DUI

"Under the influence of alcohol" is defined as having consumed an amount of alcohol that will affect the ability of the person operating a vehicle in a safe manner. Pitts v. City of Auburn, 552 So. 2d 184 (Ala. Crim. App. 1989). Initially, the police officer must have probable cause to stop or pull the Alabama citizen over then the officer may tests or evaluate you for DUI. For example, weaving, brake light out, failing to yield, tires on center or lane marker, swerving, following too closely, braking erratically, headlights off, speed slower than 10 miles per hour below limit, and signaling inconsistent with driving actions gives a police officer probable cause to stop the citizen.

After the stop, a police officer will make an observation and evaluate if the citizen smelled of alcohol, had slurred speech, had bloodshot eyes, failed field tests, and that it was the officer's opinion that the citizen was intoxicated will support the conviction for driving under the influence (DUI). Mester v. State, 755 So. 2d 66 (Ala. Crim. App. 1999). Now, let us focus on the tests you as an Alabama citizen shall be subjected too such as the breath test (breathalyzers), field sobriety test, urine test, walk and turn test, one leg stand test, horizontal gaze nystagmus (HGN), and portable alcosensor test.

Breath test (Breathalyzers)

The breath test measures the concentration of alcohol in your breathe to estimate your blood alcohol content. Breathe tests are conducted at the roadside before an arrest for DUI and is called a Preliminary Alcohol Screening test. The purpose of the Preliminary Alcohol Screening test is to help officers decide if there is probable cause to arrest you for DUI. The test can be used as presumptive evidence at trial. You will be asked to blow into a portable breath analyzer which will measure your blood alcohol content.

Can you refuse to take a DUI breath test in Alabama? You have the right to refuse a roadside breath test unless you are under 21 or on parole. It is 100% voluntary.

Should you refuse to take a DUI breath test in Alabama? Absolutely, yes you should refuse. It is in your best interests to refuse a roadside breath test because the roadside tests are not an ideal environment for conducting such tests. Also, the police officer may lack experience operating breath analyzers. Just say "No" . Ask for your lawyer.

Field Sobriety Tests

A sobriety test is a method of determining whether a person is intoxicated. <u>Black's Law Dictionary.</u> 479 (3rd Pocket ed. 2006). Specifically, a field sobriety test is a motor-skills test administered by a police officer during a stop to determine whether a suspect has been driving under the influence of alcohol. <u>Id.</u> Common field sobriety tests in Alabama are walk and turn test, one leg stand test, and horizontal gaze nystagmus test.

Walk and Turn Test

The most common DUI field sobriety test in Alabama given by police officers is the walk and turn test. A person must walk in a straight line, heel to toe, for 9 steps. The officer will then ask the person to turn and walk back in the same manner. Remember, the line may be imaginary or often the white line on the highway.

How would you know if the "walk and turn test" was given to you properly? First, the police officer must give the person clear and accurate instructions about the test. Secondly, the officer must demonstrate the act. Thirdly, the person must understand the instructions by responding to the officer's requests. Ultimately, understanding the instructions is key to passing any test. Language barriers are a major cause for misunderstanding about the test.

What conditions causes a person to fail the "walk and turn test" in Alabama? Of course, if you are drunk you are going to fail the test. However, you may also fail the test for these reasons: 1) excess weight/obesity, 2) bad eye sight, 3) over 65 years old, 4) strange shoes, and 5) any physical condition affecting balance. Always remember that field sobriety tests are not accepted in the scientific community as an accurate method to measure to measure the quantity of alcohol in a person's blood to prove the alleged DUI.

One Leg Stand Test

The "one leg stand test" is not a very scientific way of measuring intoxication. Even thought, the test is one of the common field sobriety test administered to a person. The person is instructed to stand on one leg for 30 seconds while the officer watches for balance. If the person struggles, it is reasonable to assume their blood content is 0.10 or higher. In Alabama, failing the test is a good enough reason for the officer to place you under arrest for DUI. There are five unique behaviors that the officer are evaluating: 1) hopping, 2) swaying, 3) raising arms for balance, 4) putting foot down, and 5) inability to complete test. If the person displays 2 or more of the behaviors, the person has met the criteria to be arrested and charged with Alabama DUI. The more behaviors, the more convincing the evidence is that you will be claimed to be intoxicated. However as before, the general scientific community does not accept field sobriety

tests as a measure of proving that an individual has met the
intoxication level.

Horizontal Gaze Nystagmus test

In Alabama, the "horizontal gaze nystagmus test" is an
involuntary, rapid movement of the eyes which occurs when a person
looks to the side at an object, and is characterized by an
inability of the eyes to maintain fixation as they are turned from
side to side. Holding an object such as a pen or small flashlight
about 12 inches in front of the subject' s face, the police
officer moves the object from side to side. The person is
instructed to track the movement of the object without moving his
or her head. As the test proceeds, the officer carefully observes
the subjects eyes, watching for the onset of nystagmus. The early
onset of nystagmus may be an indication that the subject has been
drinking. However, there are a great many causes for lateral gaze
nystagmus that have nothing to do with alcohol consumption. Even
further, almost everybody over the age of 40 suffers from
nystagmus to some extent.

Finger to Nose Test

In Alabama the "finger to nose test" , the police officer
evaluates the person' s physical coordination and the ability to
follow instructions. The person is required to stand erect with
eyes closed and feet together, and to touch the tip of first one
and then the other index finger to the tip of the nose. The

officer checks and records the extent of the person's success in touching the tip of the nose. Even if the person touches the tip of the nose, failure to employ the "tip" of the index finger will be graded "unsatisfactory." The officer also looks to see whether the subject remembers to close the eyes. The officer will be looking to see if your body sways back and forth plus involuntary tremors of the body and eyelids.

The Rhomberg Balance Test

In Alabama the "rhomberg balance test", the person is required to stand attention, arms at the sides, with the eyes closed and the head tilted back and to remain in that position for a stated period of time - usually 20 or 30 seconds. The officer is evaluating the person's ability to stand still without opening the eyes or raising the arms to maintain balance. The officer will be looking to see if the body is swaying in any direction, accuracy of time period assigned, and involuntary tremors of the body or eyelids.

Field Sobriety Tests (Extra information)

ALWAYS REMEMBER THAT you do not have to take the "field sobriety tests". You are not legally required to submit to the test. Unless, you certainly know that you will pass the test but you should consider to "respectfully declining" to the tests. Many people find that DUI encounter with the police dramatically increases levels of tension and anxiety, even where they have consumed no alcohol whatsoever.

The "field sobriety tests" are only one part of their capable offense against drunk driving. If a person driving displays drunken behavior, a police officer may ask the person to breathe into a portable sensor that measure blood alcohol content.

Portable Alcosensor Test

The most famous portable alcosensor is the "Breathalyzer". This instrument relies on chemical oxidation to produce the alcohol level. However, the "Breathalyzer" is being phased out for newer forms of breath testing using infrared spectroscopy technology. Common alcosensor devices are: 1) Breathalyzer, 2)Intoxilyzer, 3) BAC Datamaster, 4) Draeger, and 5) Intoximeter. Regardless of the device, these instruments rely on indirect measurements of blood alcohol content. *The accurate means of measurement is a detailed analysis of a blood sample.* It also does not measure a person's actual level of intoxication, as everyone's alcohol tolerance differs.

There are different ways to defend against a DUI charge based on an alcosensor test. Every police department has its own strengths and weaknesses that can be exposed. The temperature of the suspect, the air temperature, the users breathing pattern, the instruments calibration, among other variables affect the test's efficiency. All of these areas will be explored by your DUI attorney.   Any potential for error has been uncovered, it will be exposed in the courtroom.

Urine Test

In Alabama, when a person is arrested for a DUI, a **chemical test** is required to measure the alcohol content in the blood (BAC). The three chemical tests available are: blood, breath, and urine testing. Urine testing refers to the chemical examination of the urine in the detection of drugs or alcohol. Urine testing is generally only given as an option where a person is arrested of driving under the influence of drugs.

Of the three DUI tests, urine tests can be one of the best options for a defendant. This is because the results are often questionable. Your DUI attorney can point out the weaknesses in a urine test as grounds for your defense. A urine test does not determine the concentration of alcohol in a person's system or whether or not the person was illegally impaired. If the attorney can prove that the urine test is discredited, your DUI charge can be reduced to a reckless driving charge. If you have a reckless driving charge, you will not have to face the harsh penalties associated with a Alabama DUI charge. Higher insurance premiums, steep fines, jail, community service and alcohol education classes will no longer loom over you.

Express Your Thoughts

Express Your Thoughts

"Rarely is it advisable to meet prejudices and passions head on. Instead, it is best to appear to conform to them in order to gain time to combat them. One must know how to sail with a contrary wind and to tack until one meets a wind in the right direction."

- Fortune de Felice, 1778

Express Your Thoughts

_____

_____

_____

_____

_____

_____

_____

_____

_____

_____

"Without forgiveness there is no future."

- Desmond Tutu

Express Your Thoughts

_____

_____

_____

_____

_____

_____

_____

_____

_____

"No weapon that is formed against you shall prosper."

- Isaiah 54:17

Express Your Thoughts

"And be not conformed to this world: but be ye transformed by the renewing of your mind, that ye may prove what is that good, and acceptable, and perfect, will of God."

    – Romans 12:2

Express Your Thoughts

"People are not remembered by how few times they failed, but by how often they succeed. Every wrong step can be another step forward."

- Thomas Edison

Conclusion: Important Note from Author

Conclusion: Important Note from Author

We try to keep the information provided here up to date. However, laws often change, as do their interpretation and application. Different jurisdictions within a state may enforce the laws in different ways. For that reason, I recommend that you seek the advice of a local attorney familiar with DUI cases in your area.

In Alabama, I recommend getting a lawyer that specializes in DUI. Think positive and hope for the best. Do not let your fun night turn into a horrible experience in the judicial system.

www.ingramcontent.com/pod-product-compliance
Lightning Source LLC
Chambersburg PA
CBHW020950180526
45163CB00006B/2377